Wetlands

PETER BENOIT

Children's Press®
An Imprint of Scholastic Inc.
New York Toronto London Auckland Sydney
Mexico City New Delhi Hong Kong
Danbury, Connecticut

Content Consultant
Thomas Pypker, PhD
Michigan Technological University
Houghton, Michigan

Library of Congress Cataloging-in-Publication Data

Benoit, Peter, 1955–
  Wetlands/Peter Benoit.
      p. cm.—(A true book)
  Includes bibliographical references and index.
  ISBN-13: 978-0-531-20551-8 (lib. bdg.)   978-0-531-28100-0 (pbk.)
  ISBN-10: 0-531-20551-7 (lib. bdg.)   0-531-28100-0 (pbk.)
  1. Wetland ecology—Juvenile literature. 2. Wetlands—Juvenile literature. I. Title.
  QH541.5.M3B46 2011
  577.68—dc22   2010045936

All rights reserved. Published in 2011 by Children's Press, an imprint of Scholastic Inc.
Printed in the United States of America.
SCHOLASTIC, CHILDREN'S PRESS, A TRUE BOOK and associated logos are trademarks and/or registered trademarks of Scholastic Inc.

3 4 5 6 7 8 9 10   40   23 22 21 20 19

Find the Truth!

Everything you are about to read is true *except* for one of the sentences on this page.

Which one is **TRUE**?

T or F   Bogs are freshwater wetlands.

T or F   All wetlands are covered with water all year long.

Find the answers in this book.

Contents

THE **BIG** TRUTH!

Crocs!

Bullfrog

A hippo's bottom teeth grow
to be more than 12 inches
(30 centimeters) long.

5

Wetlands are home
to many kinds of
trees, including the
bald cypress.

CHAPTER **1**

Nature's Power

Long before people settled what is now Louisiana, the land was covered with wetlands. After heavy rains, the Mississippi River flooded the land. Floods left new soil behind, and plants thrived. Then, humans changed the land. They filled the wetlands with dirt or drained the water to make land for farms and cities. They built **levees** to keep the Mississippi from flooding. When the flooding stopped, the land began to wear away slowly.

← Swamps have trees. Marshes do not.

Hurricane Katrina

On the morning of August 29, 2005, Hurricane Katrina struck southeastern Louisiana. Fierce winds pushed rising waters over levees, and the levees crumbled. Homes filled with mud and water. Streets and entire neighborhoods were underwater. Hundreds of people died. Thousands had no place to live. Many people never returned to Louisiana.

About 80 percent of New Orleans lies below sea level.

People traveled the streets of New Orleans in boats after Hurricane Katrina.

Erosion is destroying Louisiana's coast.

A Lesson Learned

The story behind what happened to New Orleans in 2005 began in 1930. That is when engineers started building the levees. Without floods, soil lost by **erosion** was not replaced. Since 2000, Louisiana has lost more than 25 square miles (65 square kilometers) of wetlands per year. Those wetlands once protected the land from powerful storms by absorbing lots of water. With the wetlands gone, the damage from hurricanes such as Katrina is more severe.

CHAPTER 2

Squishy, Slimy, Mucky Wetlands

Wetlands are areas of land where the soil is covered with water. There are many types of wetlands. They include marshes, bogs, fens, and swamps.

A thick layer of rotting moss called peat lies under the water in this bog.

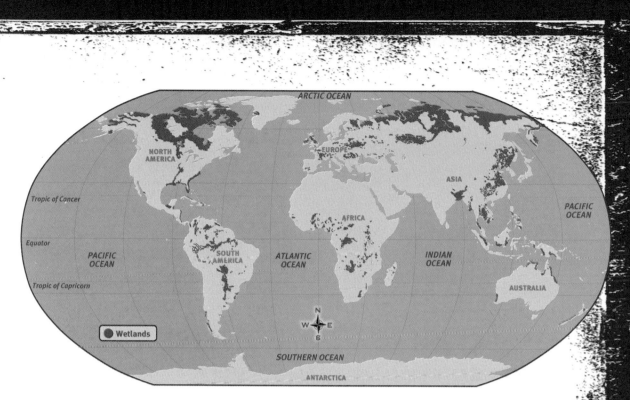

This maps shows the major wetlands on Earth.

You can find wetlands on every continent except Antarctica. They exist beside rivers and around lakes and ponds. When you walk through a wetland, the ground is squishy, slimy, and mucky.

 Bog water has so much acid that fish cannot live in it.

Mangrove trees grow to an average height of about 30 feet (9 meters).

Many wetlands plants grow partially underwater.

What Makes a Wetland?

In wetlands, water under the ground is close to the surface. When water covers this land, it does not sink into the soil because the soil is already full of water. Bogs, fens, and some swamps and marshes have freshwater. Marshes and swamps along the coast may have saltwater or a mixture of saltwater and freshwater. Some wetlands have water all year long. Others, such as prairie potholes, have water only part of the year.

Marshes

The water in marshlands may come from rivers or lakes. It may also come from ocean tides. Some marshes have both. Coastal marshes form where fresh river water meets salty ocean water. The water is shallow. Cattails, reeds, and grasses grow well. Wildflowers such as flag irises paint the edges of marshlands with yellow and blue. Ducks, geese, and pelicans flock to marshes where food is plentiful.

The American white pelican can hold 3 gallons (11 liters) of water in its bill.

Swamps

Unlike marshlands, swamps have trees. Also, the water in swamps is deeper. Most swamps have many hammocks, or areas of raised land. Red maple and live oak trees often grow on hammocks. Hammocks are formed from decaying trees. This process takes thousands of years. Cypress trees also live in swamps, but they rise out of the water. Swamps are home to many creatures, including crocodiles, bears, deer, and raccoons.

The average raccoon is about 30 to 36 inches (76 to 91 cm) long.

Raccoons hunt for berries, nuts, and eggs in North American swamps.

14

Cranberries are ready to harvest in September or October.

Cranberries are grown in bogs.

Bogs and Fens

Bogs are freshwater wetlands found in cold, **temperate** zones. There are also **tropical** bogs. Bogs get most of their water from rain and snow. Bog water has a high acid content. Fens get much of their water from small streams, rain, and underground sources. Fens are less acidic than bogs. Some fens have more **nutrients** than others. Fens rich in nutrients can support more kinds of plants. Many fens are in Canada, although there are also fens in tropical areas.

Arctic Wetlands

Bogs, fens, marshes, and swamps are all found in the Arctic regions. These wetlands are different from wetlands far to the south. When tundra snow melts in the spring, the water sits on the land's surface. Only a few inches below, the soil is frozen solid. Arctic wetlands are the nesting grounds of millions of birds. These include rare tundra swans. Other birds that nest there are ducks, geese, and cranes.

Tundra swans are also known as whistling swans.

Tundra swans have white feathers. Their young are born with pale gray feathers.

How to Build a Wetland

Beavers are fantastic builders. They build dams from trees, twigs, and branches. These dams slow the flow of stream water. The water backs up behind a beaver dam to form a pond. The land around a pond changes as water covers the ground. Reeds, grasses, and cattails grow. Insects and frogs lay their eggs in the water. Birds nest in the grasses. The beaver has made a new **ecosystem** by building its home.

Beaver dams can be as big as 16 feet (5 m) tall and 40 feet (12 m) wide.

The Okefenokee Swamp in southern
Georgia and northern Florida covers
more than 600 square miles
(1,500 sq km).

CHAPTER 3

It's All About Plants

Some wetland plants float on the surface of the water. Others grow with their roots and stems below the water's surface. Some wetland trees, such as black spruce, grow on land next to the water. The mangrove tree takes root in water. Some plants, such as cordgrass, grow in saltwater. Others, such as mallows, grow in freshwater. There are even acid-loving plants, such as sphagnum moss.

Most of the land in Okefenokee Swamp is floating islands of peat.

Floating on the Pond

A floating plant has leaves and flowers that float on the surface of still water. **Algae**, duckweed, pondweed, and water lilies are floating wetland plants. These plants provide food for ducks, geese, and fish. Floating plants also filter the water and keep it pure. Duckweed is food for humans and cattle, too. Pondweed has underwater roots, long stems, and leaves shaped like needles.

Duckweed is the world's smallest flowering plant.

Duckweed makes an excellent hiding place for some frogs.

The knobs at the base of cypress trees are called knees.

Cypress tree roots stretch deep into swamp water.

Rising Above the Swamp

Swamps are wetlands with forests. Large areas are covered with trees such as red maples, black willows, pines, and cypresses. Shrubs, such as dogwoods and alders, grow between the trees. Poison ivy loves swamps! White-tailed deer, black bears, Florida panthers, and raccoons live in swampland. Freshwater from lakes or rivers feeds some swamps. Rushes, cattails, and reeds grow along swamp edges. They provide hiding places for small animals and nesting places for wading birds.

Wapato is an American Indian name for arrowheads.

There are about 20 different species of arrowheads.

Rooted in the Water

Emergent plants have roots and stems underwater. Their leaves and flowers rise out of the water and into the sunlight. Cattails, bulrushes, and arrowheads are common emergent plants. Geese and muskrats eat cattails. Bulrushes grow in thick clumps where ducks and geese make their nests. Arrowheads, with large bulbs, are also known as duck potatoes. Birds, muskrats, porcupines, and beavers feed on these roots.

Dining on Insects

Most wetlands have poor soil. To get missing nutrients, some plants eat insects. These are called carnivorous plants because they eat meat. When an insect tickles a Venus flytrap, the plant snaps shut. Sundews and pitcher plants have sweet, sticky liquid inside. An insect flies into the flower's bowl and gets stuck. Carnivorous plants have liquids that digest insects. Most carnivorous plants live in marshes, bogs, fens, and swamps.

It takes about a half second for a Venus flytrap to close on an insect.

Crocs!

The crocodile family includes crocodiles, alligators, gharials (GER-ee-uhlz), and caimans (KAY-muhnz). Huge crocodiles hunt zebras or water buffalos. Their smaller cousins settle for fish, crabs, or shrimps. Whatever their size, crocodiles have a BIG impact on the tropical swamps and marshes they live in.

The saltwater crocodile of Southeast Asia and Australia is the world's largest crocodile. It grows up to 23 feet (7 m) long.

Crocodiles are part of the wetland cycle of life. They help plants and other animals live. Crocodile poop has nutrients that help plants grow. Birds nest in the plants. Plant eaters feed on the fruit, seeds, and stems. Birds, fish, frogs, and insects lay eggs among the reeds. Larger animals eat the smaller animals. Those animals may be eaten by crocodiles. The cycle of life continues.

The dwarf caiman is the smallest member of the crocodile family. It is about 4 to 4.5 feet (1.2 to 1.4 m) long.

Hippos spend most of
their time in the water,
but they go on land to
feed at night.

CHAPTER 4

Home, Wet Home

Wetlands are home to many different kinds of animals, some of them **endangered**. Insects, fish, and **amphibians** need wetlands for laying their eggs. Large animals, such as moose, hippos, and crocodiles, pass waste in wetlands. That waste feeds plants, which, in turn, feed other animals. Some animals are food for larger animals that hunt in the wetlands.

 Hippopotamus is a Greek word meaning "river horse."

Insects

Many insects need just the right environment for laying eggs. Wetlands provide safe hiding places and food for newborns. Dragonflies, damselflies, caddis flies, and mosquitoes use wetlands for nurseries. Bees collect nectar from wetland wildflowers. Beetles munch on tender leaves. Butterflies flutter over swamp milkweed. Wetland ecosystems are buzzing, creeping, and crawling with insect life.

Dragonflies lay their eggs in healthy wetland ecosystems.

Frogs are smooth skinned and damp.
Toads are bumpy-skinned and dry.

Bullfrogs call out to each other with loud croaking sounds.

Amphibians and Reptiles

Croaking toads sing in ponds and marshes during warm months. Bullfrogs will feed on anything they can fit in their mouths. Smaller frogs and lizards settle for insects. These amphibians share their wetland homes with turtles and lizards. Wetlands are also home to some slightly larger reptiles, including alligators, crocodiles, and snakes. Amphibians and reptiles are cold-blooded. You'll often see them resting in the sun to warm up.

Birds

Wetlands attract many different kinds of birds. Ducks, geese, and swans are waterfowl. They nest in wetlands, hiding their eggs and babies among tall reeds. Wading birds, such as cranes and storks, have long, thin legs. They stand knee-deep in water and use their long bills to peck food from the water. Songbirds also flock to wetlands. They can find plenty of berries, nuts, and insects in swamps and marshes.

Whooping cranes were near extinction. Today, whooping cranes live in Florida and Texas.

Most waterfowl live in one place in the winter and fly to another place for the summer.

Florida panthers are a critically endangered species. Only about 100 live in the wild.

Mammals

From tiny mice to massive hippos, **mammals** thrive in swamps and marshes. Predators find wetlands good places to hunt because so many animals live there. For example, a wild hog browses on roots and berries in the Everglades. A Florida panther preys on the hog. Eventually, the panther dies, and its body rots. The nutrients in the body feed the soil so that more roots and berries grow.

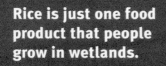

Rice is just one food product that people grow in wetlands.

CHAPTER 5

Why Wetlands Are Important

When wetlands disappear, humans suffer. Wetlands help clean waste and **pollution** from freshwater. We get fish, rice, cranberries, salt, and vegetable oil from wetlands. Some wetland plants provide the ingredients for medicines we use to keep us healthy. We weave the stems and leaves into mats and baskets. We feed the plants to cattle. People even dry moss from bogs and burn it as fuel.

Three billion people around the world depend on rice as their main food.

Swamps can handle huge amounts of rain.

Flood Control

Wetlands are used to handling water. When rains are heavy or snow and ice melt, flooding causes little harm in wetlands. The extra water raises the water level in a marsh or bog. But it does not kill the plants or wash away the soil. Hurricanes may blow down trees in swamps, but the swamps will survive. The wetlands slow the rate of soil loss. Swamps act as shields against the effects of bad storms.

Life in a Drop of Water

A drop of wetland water is filled with life. There are plants and animals we cannot see without a microscope. A drop might include algae, tiny green plants that grow by the billions in pond water. Equally tiny animals, including worms, feed on the plants. Insect young, tadpoles, and baby fish feed on the microscopic living things. The life in a drop of water is the start of a food chain that ends with human beings.

Take a look at a drop of pond water through a microscope.

Danger, Do Not Drain!

Draining water from wetlands and turning that land into farmland or towns gets in nature's way. It reduces the number and variety of plants and animals. The loss affects the quality of all life. Just over 200 years ago, the United States had about 220 million acres (90 million hectares) of natural wetlands. Today, only about 110 million acres (45 million ha) remain.

Timeline of Florida Wetland History

8000 B.C.E.
Wetlands now known as the Everglades begin forming as Ice Age glaciers melt.

1850–1860 C.E.
Florida Swamp Land Act allows people to drain the Everglades.

The Everglades

The Florida Everglades is one wetland that has been affected by draining water. People wanted to make the land available for farming and building roads and homes. The Everglades once covered about 11,000 square miles (28,000 sq km). Now it covers about 4,000 square miles (10,000 sq km).

1947
Everglades National Park is established.

2000
Rebuilding and restoring the Everglades begins.

Adult black bears weigh
200 to 600 pounds
(90 to 270 kilograms).

CHAPTER 6

Saving the Wetlands

In the past 50 years, people have learned important lessons about wetlands. Saving water, plants, and animals is important. Governments and organizations are working to protect wetland ecosystems. We cannot save endangered species unless we save their habitats. This is true for Florida black bears, butterflies, and bald eagles.

Black bears may look scary, but they usually eat roots, buds, and berries.

Fixing the Problems

By 1993, half of the world's wetlands had been drained. In the United States, laws now protect wetlands from being drained. The nation's biggest wetland project is restoring the Everglades. The state of Florida bought mangrove forests, cypress swamps, saw-grass marshes, and other wetlands from the U.S. Sugar Corporation. The company owned land that is very important to the health of the Everglades. The purchase will reduce flood problems and provide clean water for people.

Water hyacinths reproduce very quickly, allowing them to take over small bodies of water.

Wetlands provide people with places to boat and fish.

Wetlands are great places for bird-watching.

What Can We Do?

There are several things people can do to restore wetlands. First, we must stop draining water from the land. Reducing water pollution will also help. We can reduce the amount of garbage we make. How we get rid of that garbage is also important. People who use wetlands for boating or fishing must leave the area as clean as it was when they arrived.

The Cycle of Life

We know that all living things are linked together. Our lives are tied to the plants and animals in our world. In the past, people have destroyed wetlands. Now, it is time to save them. We can save bald eagles and whooping cranes. We can protect alligators and tigers. We can set aside land as national parks or wildlife preserves. It is not hard to do. Then we can all enjoy wetland ecosystems for years to come. ★

Some ducks dive deep into the water to catch food.

Protecting wetlands will help to make sure there is enough space for animals such as these ducks to live and grow.

Amount of Earth's land surface covered by wetlands: 6 percent

Amount of Earth's wetlands found in Canada: Nearly 25 percent

Year that Everglades National Park was established: 1947

Amount of wetlands remaining in the United States: Slightly more than 100 million acres (40 million ha)

Number of North American flocks of naturally migrating whooping cranes: 1

Amount of wetlands Louisiana loses every year: 25 sq. mi. (65 sq km), about 1 acre (0.4 ha) of wetlands every 33 minutes

Did you find the truth?

(T) Bogs are freshwater wetlands.

(F) All wetlands are covered with water all year long.

Resources

Books

Campbell, Andrew. *Wetlands in Danger*. Danbury, CT: Franklin Watts, 2008.

Cooper, Sharon Katz. *Marshes and Pools*. Chicago: Raintree, 2010.

Corwin, Jeff. *The Extraordinary Everglades*. New York: Grosset & Dunlap, 2010.

Johansson, Philip. *Marshes and Swamps: A Wetland Web of Life*. Berkeley Heights, NJ: Enslow, 2008.

Kalman, Bobbie, and Amanda Bishop. *What Are Wetlands?* New York: Crabtree Publishing, 2003.

Markle, Sandra. *Crocodiles*. Minneapolis: Carolrhoda Books, 2004.

Scrace, Carolyn. *Life in the Wetlands*. New York: Children's Press, 2005.

Somervill, Barbara A. *Animal Survivors of the Wetlands*. New York: Franklin Watts, 2004.

Wechsler, Doug. *Marvels in the Muck: Life in the Salt Marshes*. Honesdale, PA: Boyds Mills Press, 2008.

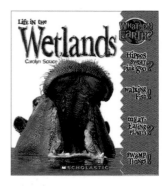

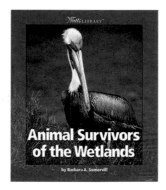

Organizations and Web Sites

Kids Do Ecology—World Biomes: Freshwater Wetlands
http://kids.nceas.ucsb.edu/biomes/freshwaterwetlands.html
Learn more about the plants and animals that live in wetlands.

Louisiana Wetlands Deal with Oil Spill—
Scholastic Kids Press Corps
www2.scholastic.com/browse/article.jsp?id=3754733
Watch a video to learn more about how the 2010 BP oil spill affected the Louisiana wetlands.

National Wildlife Federation: What's a Wetland?
www.nwf.org/Kids/Ranger-Rick/People-and-Places/
Whats-a-Wetland.aspx
Read some interesting facts about wetlands.

Places to Visit

Cuyahoga Valley National Park
15610 Vaughn Road
Brecksville, OH 44141
(800) 257-9477
www.nps.gov/mwr/cuva/
Go for a hike in this national park to get a close-up view of the wetlands.

Everglades National Park
40001 State Road 9336
Homestead, FL
33034-6733
(305) 242-7700
www.nps.gov/ever
Explore the most famous wetlands in the United States.

Important Words

algae (AL-jee) — small plants that have no roots or stems and grow on water

amphibians (am-FIB-ee-uhnz) — cold-blooded animals with backbones that have gills when young and breathe air as adults

ecosystem (EE-koh-sis-tuhm) — a community of plants and animals and the environment they live in

emergent (ee-MUR-juhnt) — plants rooted in shallow water with most of their growth above water

endangered (en-DAYN-jurd) — at risk of dying out completely

erosion (ih-ROH-zhuhn) — the gradual process of the wearing away of a substance due to the action of wind or water

levees (LEH-veez) — barriers built to prevent a river from flooding

mammals (MA-muhlz) — warm-blooded animals with backbones that feed their young with milk produced by the mother

nutrients (NOO-tree-uhntss) — substances needed by living things to stay strong and healthy, such as proteins, vitamins, and minerals

pollution (puh-LOO-shuhn) — harmful materials introduced into the air, soil, or water

temperate (TEM-pur-it) — a climate that doesn't normally have extreme high or low temperatures

tropical (TROP-uh-kuhl) — having to do with certain hot, rainy areas

Index

Page numbers in **bold** indicate illustrations

About the Author

Peter Benoit is educated as a mathematician but has many other interests. He has taught and tutored high school and college students for many years, mostly in math and science. He also runs summer workshops for writers and students of literature. Mr. Benoit has also written more than 2,000 poems. His life has been one committed to learning. He lives in Greenwich, New York.

PHOTOGRAPHS ©: cover: Jeff Rotman/Nature Picture Library; back cover: Dave Marsden/Alamy Images; 3: yurok/iStockphoto; 4: Bernhard Richter/Shutterstock; 5 top: Ryan M. Bolton/Shutterstock; 5 bottom: adam james/Alamy Images; 6: John Eastcott & Yva Momatiuk/Science Source; 8: Dave Martin/AP Images; 9: Brad Puckett/American Press/AP Images; 10: yurok/iStockphoto; 11: Jim McMahon; 12: Borut Furlan/WaterF/age fotostock; 13: TFoxFoto/Shutterstock; 14: Catcher of Light, Inc./Shutterstock; 15: DenisTangneyJr/iStockphoto; 16: Martin Fowler/Shutterstock; 17: David Hosking/Minden Pictures; 18: Jon McLean/Alamy Images; 20: DyziO/Shutterstock; 21: CrackerClips Stock Media/Shutterstock; 22: Erin Paul Donovan/Alamy Images; 23: Chris Mattison/Alamy; 24: Bernhard Richter/Shutterstock; 25: Nature's Images/Science Source; 26: adam james/Alamy Images; 28: Rob Hainer/Shutterstock; 29: Ryan M. Bolton/Shutterstock; 30: Scott E Nelson/Shutterstock; 31: Buddy Mays/Alamy Images; 32: Sia Chen How/Shutterstock; 34: Daniel Lang/Alamy Images; 35: Laguna Design/Getty Images; 36 left: Look and Learn/Bridgeman Images; 36 right: Chronicle/Alamy Images; 37 left: AP Images; 37 right: Gerhard Schulz/age fotostock; 38: Minden Pictures/Masterfile; 40: Alex Robinson/Getty Images; 41: Jerry and Marcy Monkman/EcoPhotography.com/Alamy Images; 42: Design Pics Inc/Alamy Images; 43: Martin Fowler/Shutterstock; 44: Scholastic Library Publishing, Inc.; 48: Clifford Oliver Photography.